MW01601886

Why So Insecure?

How To Overcome Emotional Insecurities Dead In Its Tracks!

By Michael S. Widmore

Michael S. Widmore

No part of this book may be reproduced or transmitted in any form whatsoever, electronic, or mechanical, including photocopying, recording, or by any informational storage or retrieval system without express permission from the author.

Copyright © 2014 JNR Publishing Group

All rights reserved.

ISBN-13: 978-1503266162

ISBN-10: 1503266168

CONTENTS

Michael S. Widmore

Other books by JNR Publishing Group

Introduction

The purpose of this book is to make you the reader fully understand what Insecurity really means by exploring its many facets in daily life. The more you understand the problem, the more you get to see the face of the enemy that is called "Insecurity".

Later on you'll be provided the means to fix yourself and possibly rewire your beliefs, emotional reactions and how you view yourself.

Insecurity is just impossible to exist, if you are solid on the inside! If you know yourself well enough- both the good and the bad- and that you can easily remedy a vast majority of your character flaws and shortcomings creating that sense of insecurity from inside of you.

What Insecure People Look Like

Insecure people constantly make an effort to establish themselves. If you are dating an emotionally insecure man, although the world loves a good joke regarding the emotional insecurities of men, the problem is quite real. In fact, it can be crippling and dangerous for your welfare. I see characteristics mentioned here in people I believe are fairly safe too so I wonder if they're insecure in certain situations just.

An insecure person has a need to make sure he or she's in the know about everything. In this sense, psychological protection may be seen as part of resilience. He feels as though his awareness of self-worth (or lack of it) is seen in the woman in his life because he will need to have sex and a woman to be happy.

But almost consistently insecurity is a trait that's associated with people who have low self esteem.

In addition they show signs of magical thinking when they accuse people by saying they're able to see into the future or read other people's minds and other nonsense.

They want to change and improve their lives, but have insecurities making it tough to achieve that aim. If you're open and willing to shake your beliefs and insecurities a little bit, if you are willing to focus on regaining the power and control over your life and establish your confidence, these measures can help you do just that.

There is an opportunity that anyone who has suffered insecurities in their lives might well become sensitive to the insecurities of others and thus become more understanding and sympathetic. Your relationships are one of many matters which your childhood insecurities can most affect. Other relationship scars, along with broken homes, the departure of a loved one could be causes.

Their insecurities can also masquerade in other forms such as noticed in tyrannical rule and their excessive living. The wearing of jewelry, makeup, and an obsession with being in style are signs of insecurities sometimes, though not necessarily so. Because of the inability to form strong attachments and learn from their role models this causes them to have issues developing emotionally (though there are a number of confounding variables here .

Vulnerable individuals are not driven by a desire to learn as they are to know whether they are better or worse from others, although we've lots to learn from other folks. Sometimes insecurities such as in this case becomes a strong source of motivation to improve. There is a silver lining to insecurity.

Self consciousness involved with insecurities is actually evidence of an excessive amount of self, pride. Insecurities will be under control, subside, vanish and go away if this particular aspect is handled.

Secure individuals make intelligent contributions naturally while insecure individuals try a bit too hard to be fascinating. Secure individuals are confident, insecure individuals will not shut up about themselves, etc to get validation from others. An unhealthy relationship is made up of two insecure people who require emotional energy. A partner that is secure understands he/she does not have to control 100% attention from his partner nor allow you to feel guilty in the event that you don't give it. That is one of the sure signs of insecurity.

Putting Others Down

Just as insecure-kind guys might criticize other people and also other groups of people, so they could put people back down to their low level.

Michael S. Widmore

Folks have insecurities not because they were exposed to a lot of happiness, encouragement and positivity but because those close to them criticized and hurt them in the past.They were exposed to destructive behaviors.

Parents form the first relationship that colors all our other relationships in life. Or maybe it's the insecurity of a bumpy relationship that keeps you up at night. And the thing about insecurities is that we are the only ones affected by them. Other people are so involved with their very own lives, in their very own stories, in their particular duties, that they aren't thinking about you as much as you believe they are looking or thinking about you.

Nervousness and insecurities are like our thoughts fooling us into thinking there is risk when there isn't. The majority of us have some insecurity, however there is a difference between being insecure of a specific facet (e.g., appearance, ability, potential risk etc.) and insecurity being inside the core of who we are - touching every part of ourselves, what we think and do.

Many people become insecure because of being occasionally bullied by family or friends at school or at work. Enough to make a substantial impact on their lives; whereas, some folks are vulnerable as a result of constant and daily abuse (e.g. verbal, physical, sexual, etc.) that last for years. Thing is, the only people that will help us avert our insecurities are ourselves.

Most Vulnerable people are content with their lives, but for those among you who wish to escape out of that prison of negativity, there is hope for you yet. When Vulnerable individuals plan their assault, Confident people counter that strike, by not acknowledging their behavior with all the expected negative response. If yourself are in a relationship and you are constantly belittling your better half because insecure people are doing great for themselves and you're not doing so well at the minute......then you are Insecure. We should be helping each other, not pulling people down!

Emotional Vampires

Lots of people never learn to produce their own mental satisfaction and continue to seek it from other people,like so called emotional vampires, carrying it even into maturity. Extreme insecurity is usually marked by means of an obsession with obtaining the acceptance of other people by any means. But irrational attention getting behaviors that is highly emotive is something to be anxious about and is a tell tale sign to be wary of.

Mental immaturity is just another cause for insecurity. Psychological security of an individual's opinion is to be distinguished from that of protection or emotional safety provided by a non-threatening, supportive environment. And, after reading this book, I am pretty sure you'll arrive at ways to eradicate insecurities.

When Insecurity Is a Good Thing

If you are unhappy with your appearance or the way you are or the life you live, it causes insecurities. Winners use it to better themselves, while the losers complain and eventually paralyzed and destroyed by it. Among the best methods to understand insecurities would be to understand the problem's root cause. If any of these causes sound familiar, analyze your heart for any resulting insecurity.

There are signs these people are indeed insecure folks. Insecure people often locate similar individuals that are as insecure. Understanding the insecurity signs is absolutely crucial before building any kind of relationship with them, so you don't get victimized yourself.

Dealing with the root of our fears and insecurities

Low self esteem and insecurities are the usual culprit that prevent us from receiving any benefits from good things that happen to us and our relationships. Things like body image, personal flaws, and other areas of our lives can cause insecurities. Identify all these areas and one by one eliminate them! You won't take them all out, but each time an area of your life is fixed, one more dead insecurity can be buried.

It's hopeless to feel perfectly secured in everything... the best thing is to understand your insecurities and work on them to the best of your ability. All of us have insecurities even those people who are already gifted with intelligence, talents, money or good looks. Just keep in mind that you're amazing inside and out!,

The Insecure vs Secure/Confident

It appears that everything individuals that are insecure do is the extreme opposite of what folks that are secure would do. Confident people are humorous, folks that are insecure crack too many jokes and with the intent of trying to gain desperate attention and affection, instead of being a value giver through good feelings and fun times from the joking.

Insecure people can even take a compliment the wrong way, instead of being thankful.
Other signals of insecurity are envy, abusiveness, possessiveness, and even over sexuality. Insecure people can still feel insecure when they've been told they're loved. There's no satisfying these people.

Girls (just like men) love all sorts of different body types. Experimenting and exploring her body can also be awesome to her ego and pride. You don't need to be insanely attractive or rich to find a relationship or love.

The Insecure Become Prey or Victims

From marketing and advertising to illegal hustling and con artistry, we are all subjected to messages and activities that agitate our own insecurities. Everyone has to have insecurities somewhere, and the more you have it, the more likely you can be manipulated. Still, it is necessary to not only detect insecurities so we can beat them to lead a fulfilled life.

It's an emotional reaction to one's failure to measure up to a particular ideal. Catastrophes, absence of successes, failures, hardships, emotional fragility, and the struggles experienced by us in life will serve to put your insecurities in focus. Yet, insecurities possess a means of forthwith re-framing your experiences so that you are deluded into thinking that you are the casualty of an unfair world dead set on bringing you down. Classic victim mentality.

Due to the proliferation of social media and Facebook, we essentially make ourselves public to the whole world- including our insecurities are magnified many folds. Share your insecurities with individuals you are attached with, they will know the best way to help you once they understand you better. Share it with the wrong people, and you can bet they will use it to push your buttons and agitate the weak sense of self that is already there.Don't share with those who will just worsen those feelings. Facebook and social media has this effect. It magnifies things we like to brag to the world, but consequently also the things we'd rather hide.

Fear Of The Unknown

Not knowing what to do, not having the answers; leads to insecurity. For instance, being financially insecure may mean just making enough to cover the rent, which causes stress, and could lead you to worry getting kicked out. Humans like to feel covered against any contingencies and problems. Acceptance of the unknown, being at peace that it is part of life is the way to defend against such fears.

Positive Self Image And Attitude

Insecurity isn't an objective assessment of a person's skill but an interpretation that is emotional and subjective. As two people with the same abilities may have entirely various levels of fear or insecurity. Among the symptoms of a mental episode from a tripped insecurity is the inability to maintain positive outlook in life, or another is living up the "hype" they themselves created. Especially, people who are misusing the social media tools given to them and creating false beliefs of themselves that are fueling their very own insecurities, together with the insecurities cause by their peers.

While you may believe someone is faking insecurity for attention (common dramas in facebook lol), they may have emotional or mental difficulties you're not aware of. Try not to assume just because you are able to see no apparent defects in their life, that someone is faking insecurity. As mentioned previously, it is subjective! It doesn't matter if its true or not, just that the person believes them to be!

Not being able to curb anxieties and insecurities can make difficulties, or sabotage any kind of relationship. As you mature your perspective on your own insecurities may be altered through experience.

Appreciating the insecurities of another can let you relate with them better and additionally, it may help you to ward off the less thoughtful things that folks occasionally say or do to us. Those who are hurt, tend to do hurtful things too.

Handle The Different Causes Of Insecurities In Your Life

An insecurity that is about feeling vulnerable about your skills at speaking lets say, is quite different than an insecurity about your ability to make money. There are many types of insecurities and each one deserves to be looked and treated individually. Be objective about aspects of yourself and make improvements accordingly to each one. Insecurities can be caused by a lot of things, as pointed out, the significant idea isn't to let them rule your life, instead serve as impetus to help reduce your flaws.

I believe when our expectations of ourselves and the sensed or spoken views of others do not align, insecurities are the end result.

Our self perception about our capabilities are distorted by insecurities, These insecurities alter our behaviors and activities which ultimately change our life for the worse.

Insecurities Affect How We View Others And Ourselves

We become competitive and constantly compare ourselves to others; occasionally we become judgmental to make ourselves feel exceptional. Inferiority complexes oftentimes develop when we compare ourselves to others, and fall short of their so called caliber. Unfortunately insecurities and low -self image leads to other negativities such as, animosity, envy, backbiting, rage, ungratefulness, and arrogance which further makes things worse!

Financial Related Insecurities

Being on a tight budget doesn't mean that you can't give your partner, relative, friend etc a good time. If the company you keep are looking at your bank account more than your personality, then you must stop being with these shallow, materialistic people and choose those who can appreciate you, and not what you have.

Many have been shoved into self-employment because they can't find a suitable alternative occupation (with the recession and all).

Throughout history, men have become the one tasked with being providers. But long-term job insecurity has forced many to reevaluate personal priorities, lifestyle changes and as a result their egos are hit, and thus causing financial related insecurities.

Guys especially feel insecure when they do not make enough cash and fear that he is perceived as a failure if he is not on a six digit salary.

Food insecurity means families do not have enough cash to consistently get all the food they need on a regular basis. This is especially much worse than the insecurity of not having money for the kids' tuition and other needs. This can be devastating for parents self esteem too!

The more money a guy makes the better he is as a man, speaking from a evolutionary point of view and typical role of a man.

Being out of work with no cash will certainly cause anyone to feel insecure. Those experiencing career transitions have problems coping with their internal world while in between jobs.

How to Stop Being Insecure Then?

You should find out the best way to stop being insecure and the best way to stop being paranoid. Easier said than done how one can quit feeling vulnerable all the time. There isn't going to be a stop to it for some. The human mind by its own very nature is constantly insecure.

Some even resort to taking drugs just to cease feeling insecure all the time and eliminate stress.

Telling someone they need to simply quit being insecure is pointless. All of this is not to say that we all should atleast find ways to feeling insecure all the time.

When the root causes can be found and you can remove them or come to terms with them, you can just start feeling less and less affected by it. Which is often an immense cause for confidence increase. It's important to consider the causes behind your anxieties and insecurities; subsequently take action to eliminate the root problems as mentioned earlier. You got to be patient and provide help not only in uncovering the root causes, but in overcoming the insecurities .

Beliefs in higher power

Faith in God is one of the better ways to quit feeling vulnerable and fearful all the time.
If all of the signs are pointing towards a favorable scenario, an insecure man without faith,will likely deny it all only to remain on their course that is ill-fated. He's just given up on a better future! What that individual needs is to regain trust in himself, in the world, and get his faith back! That things will be alright.

Do efforts to assist yourself to grow in all facets of life, from health and love to designing a better lifestyle, improving your career and achieving your life's goal. That'll make you to feel a lot more protected, and have a sense of purpose because there is a higher power, or sense of destiny at play. If you can not handle your insecurities, and if it feels overpowering, there is no shame

Michael S. Widmore

in asking for help from God, family, friends, even Psychotherapists if necessary.

Men's Insecurities

Guys who have no cash are made to feel inadequate. You can not blame men who have no money, cash has become a tremendous factor in the male-female game. The male obviously desires to be that guy not only with the fancy car, thick wallet, a mansion in Beverly hills with the killer abs, and gets all the girls go nuts over his six pack and Greek god looks. But we cant all be like that.

Bring up the topic of hair loss especially if his dad is now balding and he can get extremely touchy.

Men are also insecure about their heights because deep down, they understand it matters, on a fundamental level (from an evolutionary point of view). Truthfully, though, that there is a tremendous edge (for guys) if thy are big and intimidating looking. Imagine how much more assurance it requires for all the short guys out there to come up and attempt to speak with a taller woman, when everybody knows that nearly every girl listing qualities she wants in a man normally begins with 'tall!'.

This makes the effort to beat your body insecurity or negative body image all the more significant. Face up to ourselves with all our imperfections and insecurities. Make friends, start dating and forget about your insecurities. Even those you believe have it all still have their very own insecurities. Remember no one is perfect!

A guy that is quite secure will not be concerned about what other guys think and say about him. The secure man is not afraid to be in touch with his feelings because he understands the value of emotions, and that it will not communicate that he's not strong or feminine.

Confident men are happy with themselves and can simply adore the other person for who they are. Guys who put you down and criticize you and are just plainly insecure.

On the other hand an insecure girl who's seeking continuous validation from others relies on her sexuality as a crutch. Guys become violent from the necessity to control their woman's flirting. That may or may not be justified all the time. Sometimes the woman is being a woman, playing her games to feel wanted by making her man jealous. But sometimes this jealousy or insecurity is justified.

Men can have some important sexual insecurities too. Impotence, premature ejaculation, a deformed body part, beer belly, even the size of his penis.

From a girls perspective, dating a clingy/ insecure man is just dead weight. To say an insecure guy is going isolate the woman from friends and family to rope her in, mistreat and suffocate her, so that she can not leave and lock the door is simply idiotic.

In case the woman is put in a relationship with an insecure guy, she'll need to spend all her time trying to please him and make him feel happy and fulfilled in the relationship. One of the easiest methods to recognize an insecure guy is when his woman is having a nice conversation with another guy , by watching his behavior he is over protective, jealous and just does not understand why the women is in a relationship with him. Because she chose him among other men!

It's the troubled guys who simply cannot manage it. These are the guys who are uncertain of themselves who constantly second guess themselves especially if they're dating a top caliber woman i.e out of his league..

The more insecure you are, the more that insecurity weighs on your mind. Many guys (and gals) have insecurity, it is all a question of how you deal with it and let it affect you. A man simply doesn't have as much leeway to be insecure than a woman does. A woman should be able to rely on his man to be his emotional center, to be her rock, to be her source of strength!

Relationship Insecurities

One of the most effective methods to really get relationship insecurities would be to dissect the root cause of the problem. Whether we like to acknowledge it or not, we all have insecurities of one type or another. A fantastic way to begin this procedure would be to share your insecurities with those who overcame their body insecurities and thrived! In the areas of love and dating, it doesn't take a lot of effort to find very successful guys in the seduction game, who are neither tall, rich, good-looking and all that jazz. They faced up to their limitations and overcame it! They trained themselves to be so amazing, they are able to defeat guys who have it all, in spite of having nothing but a great personality and game.

In the meantime do your best not to be needy, insecure and insane with your lover and how you handle the relationship. For instance, you definitely would like to quit calling your partner too much, start envisioning the feeling of calmness, oozing self-confidence and make your self respect grow.

There actually is just one way of ridding yourself of things that make you feel insecure. Live through anything you're scared of and just put yourself out there. Those people who experience little insecurities on the other hand could be better off by taking more risks and experience more of life. Behave like you understand something they are not privy to because they like to play it safe all the time.

It's not impossible to work on your own insecurities by learning to maintain and stand up on your own 2 feet, asking yourself questions about the very things that cause unrest, and maintaining a journal of your day-to-day ideas, conquests and systematic destruction of the insecurities.

Strive to become less defensive, more objective, more serene, and open to your partner's viewpoint. Beating insecurities is no simple task, but it can be treated.

When you defeat these insecurities, and confess to your own

insufficient self-confidence in your financial or sexual abilities, as an example, these elements of your life will turn to good things, after the dragons have been slain.

There are powerful strategies to handle the mental and emotional spikes that induce us to behave irrationally in the face of insecurities.

If you have problems with various insecurities one thing you could do is to start to focus upon the opposite qualities you need to develop. It is powerful as it helps to reprogram your responses and behaviors with the cause of insecurities as well as the symptoms.

Quit when you find yourself doing it (bad behavior). Therefore, in the event you want to cease being insecure, you must do the opposite and artificially get into that feeling or state of being totally assured and confident etc. It is difficult in the beginning to feel the exact opposite-but with training you can do it. The insecurity response is a learned or conditioned response which you can UNtrain.

Learning to Trust

Your power to trust others can enhance your actual relationships and how you handle or treat your personal insecurities .

Bitterness and envy are relationship killers. It's a fact that before you can really be fulfilled within an intimate relationship, you must learn how to fulfill and love yourself.

You are insecure as you do not believe you are good enough. Figure out how to manage it by talking and working these issues together with your partner. Be exhaustive and list each and every one thing that's causing these problems.

You also need to make an effort to beat the insecurities instead of concealing them. Don't hide or run away from it, FACE IT! Mental control is when a person has full command over his emotional and psychological faculties.

Fragile Sense Of Self

Needless to say there are innumerable distinct variables that constantly reinvent our self images as well as our mental health, both environmental and genetic.After you have located the cause of the issue, it is much more easy to get a handle on the insecurity, since it was most probably created by a couple of isolated cases which have no actual value in your present life, but still managed to define your self image. For example, just because you failed at your first business venture doesn't mean you're a failure! On the contrary, successful businessmen failed much more than they succeeded. But someone with a fragile sense of self will make those causations and conclusions.

It's Just Part Of Life

Insecurity is a part of life, and you will already be feeling better when you quit feeling insecure about your insecurity! It's just part of the deal of being human in this planet. Know that some insecurities I must face and defeat, some are out of my control and that I should understand to simply cope and accept them. In a sense, feel secure that you have insecurities, because it's about as sure as the sun rises and sets, and that someday we'll die. No biggie, its just part of life.

Although kids up to age 10 do not comprehend "insecurity" as a term or an emotional feeling, they start being conditioned by society and their peers to feel it as they grow.

Do not attempt to be that 'perfect picture of yourself' you have in mind, be yourself. The higher level the individual is, the higher the insecurity will be. Such is the case with supermodels who are afraid of the next top model who'll steal their spot. On the other hand, those not blessed with looks are also insecure of their looks! How can that be? That's because as mentioned repeatedly, its in our nature to always feel insecure about something!

Low self esteem is generally one of the main cause of insecurity and nervousness issues.

I can definitely say that with certain actions and appropriate words you may also make any girl (super model or common woman) feel vulnerable and insecure.. Many insecurities linger on long after the initial cause becomes nonexistent. You'd be surprised how many beautiful women were once "ugly ducklings", or just had cosmetic surgeries or just afraid to grow wrinkly as they age.

No matter your specific insecurities chance are, take time to look at the remainder of the human race and how your insecurities pale in comparison to the suffering others face. Learn to count your blessings and make the insecurity insignificant in the bigger picture.

Once self acceptance is understood, folks certainly will have a favorable prognosis for the future and will shy away from insecurities.

Relationship Insecurities

When one partner has a tendency to be too possessive or when a couple keeps arguing over something similar that happened before, it is high time to reassess the relationship and uncover the main causes of the feelings that are causing insecurity. Paradoxically our current behavior is determined by our past, and causes us to live in anxiety even though there's no actual reason to be fearful in our present day life.

Do this in bits (going slowly, with little activities, building toward the entire activity that causes the anxiety) and finally, this retrains the head to have the ability to feel trust or whatever desired emotional state, once more. Understand it will become more manageable in time as you practice.

Unless the insecurities are linked to things which are now occurring in your relationship and about them, you telling them that you are insecure because an ex did something in the past will simply let them know that you are not over this whole thing yet. You pretty much need to do some growing up!

Insecurities can induce you to despise other people or handle them with hostility, rudeness, dishonor and disrespect.

On one hand, your partner may continue doing the things which make you feel insecure and may believe you are making a big deal out of nothing. Your insecurities are encompassing. They define how you socialize with others, therefore it is critical before you repair anything else to repair yourself- because all these things may just be in your head.

For a number of people, leaving insecurities behind may be demanding to do. However, it could be done, and it starts with having faith in your abilities and your partner. To have faith in this relationship.

Many of us set our whole life on hold for the guarantee of love and so we remain in bad relationships that frequently causes further self-esteem problems that are more profound. That which we normally deal with in relationships is psychological insecurity, which is understood to be an unease or nervousness because one party feels undeserving or a sense of worthlessness to be dating him/her! Being stuck in a insecure relationship is not better than having just any relationship.

You must determine in the event you would like to be in a relationship, if this is the right person, if this is the right time, and if you are truly mature enough to be in one! Don't just get into one, for the sake of being in one.

Maltreatment is where insecurity becomes incredibly damaging. Know how to identify it, and eject once you see it!

There is no requirement for all of us to divulge information about ourselves or to blurt out our insecurities to our partners. However due to our insecurities we might find it hard to express and nurture love. There is a barrier preventing us from making a deep connection!

By doing this you are making actual and deep connection to address your insecurities directly rather than by attempting to conceal them. It's our duty to learn so that it won't control our own lives, rather how to control these insecurities.

Also be aware that despite this ethereal feeling of love intoxication, strong insecurities finally result in broken relationships when it is due to aggressiveness, substance and alcohol abuse, being distant and forms of maltreatment

No significant relationship will constantly work flawlessly on a regular basis. Obviously , this does not mean that you need to accept everyone into your life who's willing to take you for granted, even if they're clearly not appropriate for you But it does mean that if there are occasional problems in your relationships, you can work it out.

Conclusion

Now that you understand the many facets of Insecurities by now you should realize that most of it exists only in our minds! If you don't put attention or focus into it, no one else will! The strong are the ones who accept their flaws and not let it affect them. The strong not only undermine those self esteem feelings, but proactively addresses them so that in fact, they are becoming better, and thus less reasons to be insecure about anything!

Misery loves company. The more insecure you are, the more you attract similar negative thinkers in your life, and thus progressing this mind virus of insecurity, worsening everyone!

For the Positive people in the world? Insecurities are a major turn off, and you'll be looked down as dead weight if you ruin the positive vibes with your negativities.

There are many tools available to fix one's insecurities. It is beyond the scope of this book, but you may use tools like Sedona Method, EFT, CBT, Self Hypnosis, Affirmations, NLP (discussed in our other books published by JNR publishing), or you can do research yourself.

If you liked this book, please consider leaving a positive review so that others may gain the same insights and knowledge that could also help them!

I do not have an advertising budget, so support in the form of positive word of mouth from people like you would be immensely appreciated!

Thank you for buying this book and till the next time!

Michael S. Widmore

This guide is not intended as and may not be construed as an alternative to or a substitute for professional business, mental counseling, therapy or medical services and advice.

The authors, publishers, and distributors of this guide have made every effort to ensure the validity, accuracy, and timely nature of the information presented here. However, no guarantee is made, neither direct nor implied, that the information in this guide or the techniques described herein are suitable for or applicable to any given individual person or group of persons, nor that any specific result will be achieved. The authors, publishers, and distributors of this guide will be held harmless and without fault in all situations and causes arising from the use of this information by any person, with or without professional medical supervision. The information contained in this book is for informational and entertainment purposes only. It not intended as a professional advice or a recommendation to act.

No part of this book may be reproduced or transmitted in any form whatsoever, electronic, or mechanical, including photocopying, recording, or by any informational storage or retrieval system without express permission from the author.

© Copyright 2014, JNR Publishing

Date of publication November 17, 2014

All rights reserved.

Michael S. Widmore

Other books by JNR Publishing Group

The Seduction Force Multiplier 1- Bring Out Your FULL Seduction powers through the Power of Routines, Drills, Scripting and Protocols

The Seduction Force Multiplier 2 - Scripts and Routines Book

The Seduction Force Multiplier 3- PUA Routines Memory Transplant Package

The Seduction Force Multiplier 4 - Situational PUA Scripts and Routines

Michael S. Widmore

The Seduction Force Multiplier V - Target Auto Response Package

The Seduction Force Multiplier VI - PUA Innergame, Mindsets and Attitudes

Shielded Heart - How To Stop Yourself From Falling For A Seduction Target

How To Cheat Proof Your Relationships

Secrets to Hacking Your Brain- Be Your Own Therapist

Michael S. Widmore

Hypno Machines - How To Convert Every Object In Your Environment As a Device For Psychological and Emotional Manipulator

The Art Of Virtual Practice 2 - Learning and Mastery Of Any Skill At Lighting Speeds!

How to Operate with Your Full Potential and Talents

How To Master Resilience And Be Invincible To Life's Disappointments And Failures

The X-Factor Manual - ***Learn How To be A Model Even If You Don't Look Like One***

Michael S. Widmore

<u>The Age Erase System - Hypnotic Anti Aging Serum</u>

<u>Develop Insane Self Confidence and Naturally Unleash The Supermodel Within</u>

<u>The Persuaders Guide To Eliminating Resistance And Getting Compliance</u>

The Art of Invisible Compliance - How To Make People Do What You Want Effortlessly

Unstoppable and Fearless - Know What You Want and Get It

Michael S. Widmore

Just Go- Having The Courage and Will to Pursue Your Dreams

How To Make Better Life Decisions

How To Diet Like a Machine- Make Any Diet Program Work With Ease

Friends into Lovers: Escape and Never be Trapped In The Friendzone Ever Again!

The Permanent Anti-jealousy Solution

Michael S. Widmore

<u>*The TEN Game Operations Manual:*</u> <u>*How To Get Extremely*</u>
<u>*Gorgeous 10s Consistently and Predictably!*</u>

<u>*How Not To Give a Shit!: The Art of Not Caring*</u>

Perfecting Your Game: How To Reach Mastery Through Perfection Of Game!

Manipulative Eye Contact Techniques: Install thoughts and feelings just with your eyes!

Michael S. Widmore

The Injector Protocol: How To Inject Your Essence Literally Into Everything!

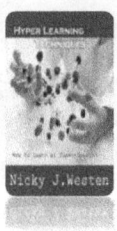

Hyper Learning Techniques: How To Learn at Super Speeds!

The Anti-AA Eradication System : **100% Foolproof Approach Anxiety Elimination Techniques and**

Protocols To Enable You To Start Approaching Dozens of Women Today!

The Ultimate Dog Training Crash Course

Maximized Energy = Maximized Potential: How to pursue the most difficult tasks with your maximum energies and potential!

Michael S. Widmore

!

<u>*Tough Love: Surviving and Winning The Most Difficult Romance Games, Relationships and Lovers From Hell!*</u>

<u>*Acting and Comedy Techniques for Seducers and PUAs*</u>

Putting Mind Control In Your Daily Life

Seducing the UNseduceable Man: Specialized seduction techniques for the impossible to get man!

Michael S. Widmore

<u>*Be A Human Lie Detector: Detect High-Level, Covert Communications of Persuaders, Seducers and Other Manipulators!*</u>

<u>*2- Styles of Communications:Perfectly calibrated communications everytime!*</u>

Techniques on Developing Irresistible Charisma at Work: A tactical-manual on how to be the ultimate People-person everyone likes and follows!

The Ultimate Guide On Manufacturing REAL Luck

Proven Strategies To Taking Control Of Your Life By Creating Your Own Luck!

Michael S. Widmore

Imitate, Innovate and Annihilate! How to Clone And Improve On competitors' Best Products and Services Effectively!

How To Increase Reputation and Popularity! Applying Practical Brand Management Principles For Businesses and Individuals

The Ultimate Business Competition Guide: Reverse Engineer The competition and Make 'em eat your dust!

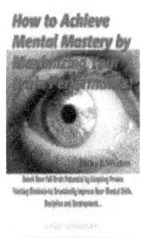

How to Achieve Mental Mastery by Maximizing Your Brain Performance!

Reach Your Full Brain Potential by Adopting Proven Thinking Methods to Drastically improve Your Mental Skills, Discipline and Development

Michael S. Widmore

<u>*Develop Irresistible Skills of Persuasion, Motivation and Leadership at Work And With Friends!*</u>

Learn the fine art and science of persuasion and motivation to effectively influence people...

<u>*The Ultimate Guide On How to Be Naturally Persuasive*</u>

Influence People Without Manipulative Persuasion Tactics and Strategies

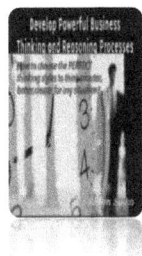

Develop Powerful Business Thinking and Reasoning Processes

How to choose the PERFECT thinking styles to think smarter, better, clearer for any situation!

The Ultimate Guide to Developing a High Performance Mentality

Michael S. Widmore

How to achieve anything you want by thinking like an Overachiever!

The Ultimate Guide to Counselling, Coaching and Mentoring

The Handbook of Coaching Skills and Tools to Improve Results and Performance Of your Team!

The Ultimate Guide on Developing Conflict Resolution Techniques for Workplace Conflicts

How to develop workplace positivity, morale, communications.

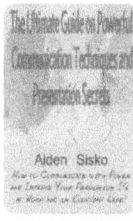

The Ultimate Guide on Proven Communication Techniques and Presentation Secrets

How to Communicate with Power and Improve Your Persuasion IQ at Work and in Everyday Life!

The Corporate Warriors Manual

Applying Military Principles to Conquer Business and Life!

The Ultimate Burnout Cure

Re-ignite your passions in life and work!

The Winner's Code

How to unleash the winner within

Michael S. Widmore

Maximizing Results Through Minimalism

Get the most out of life by focusing only on the essentials!

The Ultimate Guide To Executing Strategies, Plans & Tactics

Practicing the Art of Execution

The Ultimate Collaboration & Synergy Guide

How to bring out the best performance and results from everyone!

Being the Action-Man in Business

How to start making things happen today!

Hit the Ground Running in Business

Learn Must-know Business Fundamentals for the New Entrepreneur

Conflicting Views

Tactfully handle any conflicts in any organization

The Ultimate Guide on Developing Patience

Be a better leader by expanding your patience!

Designing & Projecting Powerful First Impressions

Pragmatic Time Management Techniques

Getting things done on time, everytime!

The Fine Art of Decision Making

Make things happen by making the right calls!

The Ultimate Guide to Building & Managing the Perfect Team

Parenting and Disciplining Strong-Willed Children

Advanced parenting techniques for defiant children!

Advanced Parenting Techniques of Rebellious Teens

The ultimate guide to parenting difficult teens from hell!

The E.Q. Genius

Mastering Emotional Intelligence

The Ultimate Guide to the Placebo Effect

Michael S. Widmore

Understanding and exploiting Placebo effects in health & life!

Mastering Creativity and Inspiration

Cures to your Creativity Problems Revealed!

The Ultimate Guide to Developing Belief in Yourself

The Inner and Outer Games of Developing Trust and Belief in your Capabilities!

Dealing With Horrible Bosses

How To Handle Bad Managers at Work

Just in your head

How to eliminate panic and anxiety disorders

How to handle tough situations

Finding Inner Strength to survive the toughest crisis and life challenges

Using the Laws Of Attraction in Sex, Love, Dating & Relationships

Exploit LOA to get what you want!

Books Available Soon

The Pet Whisperer

Teach Yourself To Communicate With Your Beloved Pets & Animals

The Ultimate OCD Self Help Book

Cure Obsessive Compulsive Disorders Once and For All!

The Mind of Swindlers, Con Men, Fraudsters & Scam Artists

Learn to Scam-proof your life!

My Buddy is `FEAR'

Using your own fear to get things done!

The Seducer's Guide To Developing A Good Sense Of Humor

Be Sexy & Funny, Without Being a Dancing Monkey!

The Art of Risk Management

Learn to Manage Risks Like a Pro

Michael S. Widmore

You Are Your Own Worst Enemy

How To Stop Self Sabotaging Behaviors Once and For All!

Make Your Own Affirmations, Autosuggestions and Self Hypnosis Products

Drastically Improve ANY Aspect of Your Life On Autopilot!

How to Fail Your Way to Success

Use Failures to Weed Out the Duds

Taming the Beasts

The Ultimate Guide How To Handle Difficult People

Layman's Guide to NLP Modelling

How to be anything you want to be!

The Child Whisperer

Persuasion Techniques to make children want or hate anything you want

Healthy Sweet Tooth

50 quick and easy mouth-watering healthy desserts to satisfy your cravings

CPSIA information can be obtained
at www.ICGtesting.com
Printed in the USA
BVHW031706120121
597662BV00001B/68